WHAT CAN WE DO?

DISEASE

ALEX WOOLF

Published in 2025 by Cavendish Square Publishing, LLC
2544 Clinton Street, Buffalo, NY 14224

First published in Great Britain in 2023 by Hodder & Stoughton

Website: cavendishsq.com

Editor: Alex Woolf
Series Designer: Dan Prescott

Picture acknowledgements:
Alamy: Pictorial Press Ltd 21t, Mile 91/Ben Langdon 23. Getty: Focus on Sport 12. Shutterstock: Johnny Bravoo 4, xuanhuongho 5, Ground Picture 6, Sergey Mironov 7, create jobs 51 8, michelmond 9, pixelheadphoto digitalskillet 10, Dario Lo Presti 11, LightField Studios 13t, Saurav022 13b, Iren_Geo 14, Nataly Gejdos 15t, Massimo Loi 15b, Martchan 16, Deliris 17, Ninc Vienna 18, Cryptographer 19t, Egoitz Bengoetxea 19b, fusebulb 20, Komsan Loonprom 21b, Jarun Ontakrai 22, Mongkolchon Akesin 24, spotters_studio 25, AnupongTermin 26, Michael Zysman 27, Kateryna Kon 28, Oluwafemi Dawodu 29t, Lightitup 29b.

All design elements from Shutterstock.

Cataloging-in-Publication Data

Names: Woolf, Alex, 1964-.
Title: Disease / Alex Woolf.
Description: Buffalo, NY : Cavendish Square Publishing, 2025. | Series: What can we do? | Includes glossary and index.
Identifiers: ISBN 9781502673794 (pbk.) | ISBN 9781502673800 (library bound) | ISBN 9781502673817 (ebook)
Subjects: LCSH: Diseases--Juvenile literature. | Public health--Juvenile literature.
Classification: LCC R130.5 W78 2025 | DDC 616.07'9--dc23

CPSIA compliance information: Batch #CW25CSQ: For further information contact Cavendish Square Publishing LLC at 1-877-980-4450.

Printed in the United States of America

CONTENTS

WHAT IS DISEASE?

When you hear the word "disease," what do you think of? You might think of measles, cancer, or Covid-19. They are all diseases, but the definition is broad. A disease is anything that harms us that hasn't been caused by physical injury. Usually a disease has a known cause and a set of symptoms (signs) that help doctors diagnose (identify) it.

Changing meaning

The word "disease" first appeared in the 14th century and it meant "lack of ease or comfort," as in "dis-ease." By the 1500s, it had gained its modern meaning. However, our understanding of disease has widened since then. For example, in those days, back pain and a stooped posture in elderly people were seen as a natural part of aging. Today, we recognize them as symptoms of the disease osteoporosis.

Keeping active as you age can help ward off diseases such as osteoporosis.

How disease affects us

Diseases upset the working of our bodies. They can make us unable to work, study, play, or enjoy life. Some diseases are communicable (they can be passed on to other people). Others are non-communicable (they can't be passed on).

How disease affects society

Diseases don't only affect us as individuals, they affect the whole of society. People who are sick or disabled because of disease may not be able to contribute to society by working, volunteering, or paying taxes. Family members may need to care for them. The more people there are suffering from disease, the greater the strain on our healthcare systems. It is therefore in everyone's interests to try to reduce or eradicate disease. Medical science is making great progress in understanding the causes of disease and developing treatments for it.

IT'S A FACT

Disease was responsible for 92.39% of all deaths worldwide in 2019. About 74.36% were from non-communicable diseases, and 18.03% were from communicable diseases.

This is a crowded hospital waiting room. Millions miss work each day due to disease.

NON-COMMUNICABLE DISEASES

Non-communicable diseases (NCDs) are diseases that are not caught through contact with other living things. Each year, NCDs kill around 41 million people and they are the leading cause of death worldwide. People with NCDs tend to live with these conditions for a long time.

Causes

NCDs may be caused by a number of different factors, including vulnerability to certain diseases inherited from your parents, exposure to air pollution, and unhealthy lifestyle choices. These include smoking, poor diet, excessive consumption of alcohol, and physical inactivity. Many elderly people suffer from NCDs, but younger people do too. Each year 17 million people die of NCDs before the age of 70.

The most deadly kinds of NCDs are cardiovascular diseases, cancer, diabetes, and chronic respiratory diseases. Between them, these four groups of diseases account for over 80 percent of all premature (early) NCD deaths.

Unhealthy diets cause malnutrition and obesity, which can lead to NCDs such as type 2 diabetes, cardiovascular disease, and some cancers.

Poorer countries

Of those who die each year from NCDs, the great majority (31.4 million) are from low- and middle-income countries. People living there are more at risk of being exposed to harmful products or live and work in polluted environments. Also, access to healthcare tends to be more restricted.

Preventing NCDs

NCDs are damaging to society and hold back the development of poorer countries. We can help reduce deaths from NCDs by taking steps to detect and treat these diseases early, by educating people on making better life choices and by taking action on air pollution. The World Health Organization (WHO) is playing a key role in coordinating and promoting the global fight against NCDs.

What Can I Do?

Young people, like all age groups, are vulnerable to NCDs. You can reduce the risk of developing an NCD by taking regular exercise and eating a healthy, balanced diet. Eat plenty of fresh fruit and vegetables and cut down on sugary snacks and drinks and foods that are high in salt.

Regular exercise helps prevent and manage NCDs. Up to five million deaths a year could be avoided if people were more physically active.

CANCER

Cancer is an NCD in which some of the body's cells divide uncontrollably and spread to other parts of the body. It can happen almost anywhere in the body. Cancer was responsible for nearly 10 million deaths (or almost one in every six people who died) worldwide in 2020. Today, thanks to new treatments, cancer is becoming much more survivable.

What causes cancer?

Genes are units within our body's cells that control how much and how often our cells divide, among many other things. Sometimes the genes get damaged or lost while the cells are dividing. This is called a mutation. As a result, the cells might divide too much, forming a lump called a tumor. Mutations can happen by chance, or by things coming from outside the body, like the chemicals in tobacco smoke. Some people can inherit faults in certain genes from their parents, making them more likely to develop a cancer.

Tumors can be detected with scans that look inside the body.

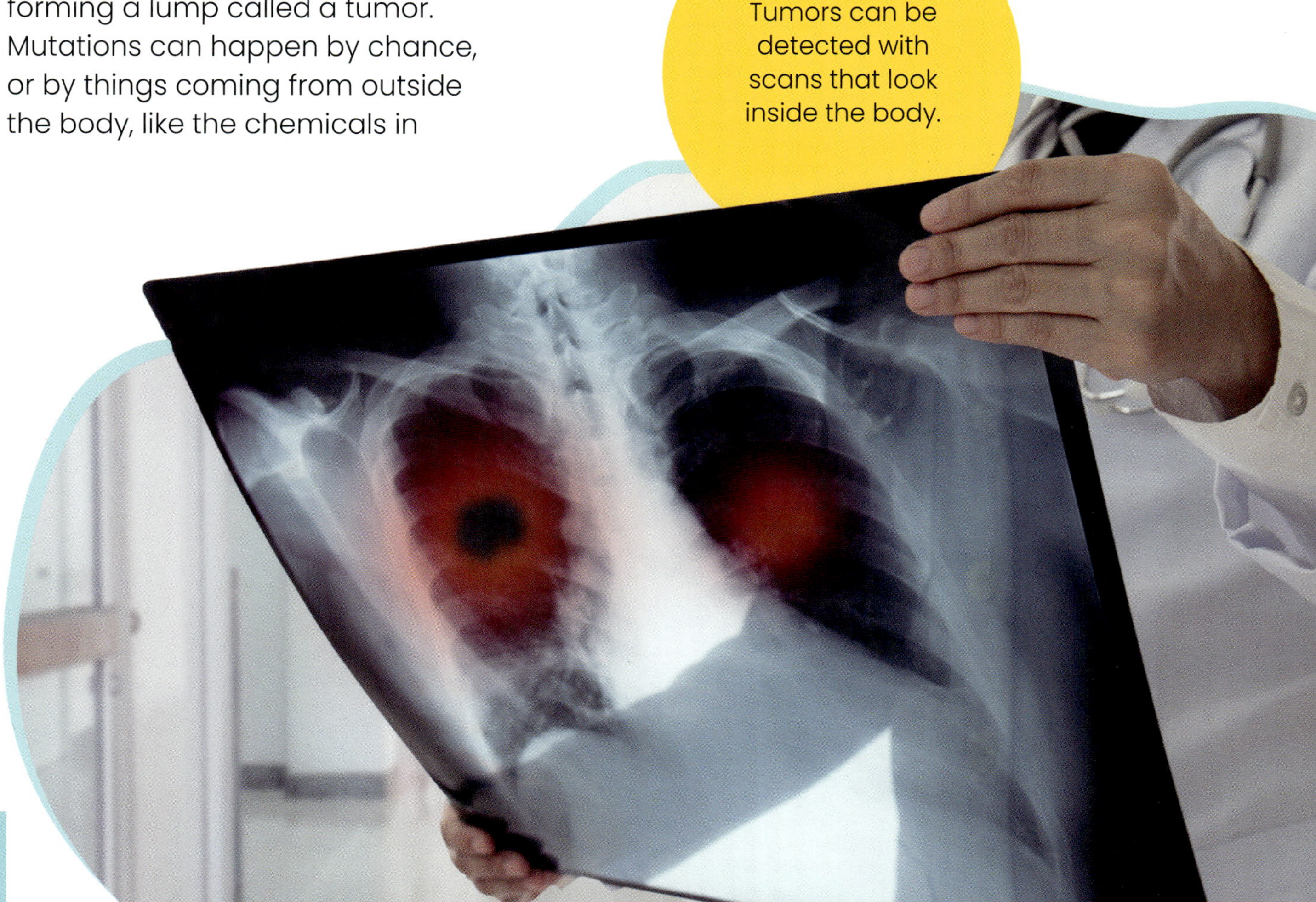

How cancer spreads

Tumors can spread to surrounding tissues, causing damage. Sometimes cancer cells spread to other parts of the body in the bloodstream or the lymphatic system. Here they can grow into new tumors. This is called metastasis. We name cancers according to where they start in the body. Common forms include breast, lung, prostate, bowel, skin, and liver cancer.

This is a race in Houston, Texas, to raise money for cancer research.

Treatment and prevention

Cancer may be treated with surgery, where surgeons cut out tissue containing cancer cells; chemotherapy, where the patient takes medicines that shrink or kill cancer cells; and radiation therapy, where high-energy rays are used to kill cancer cells. People can reduce chances of getting cancer by keeping a healthy weight, avoiding tobacco and alcohol, protecting their skin from too much sunlight, and getting tested regularly. Thanks to advances in detection and treatment, cancer survival rates are improving globally.

GLOBAL INITIATIVE FOR CHILDHOOD CANCER

Every day, more than a thousand children are diagnosed with cancer. Survival rates are only 15-45 percent for those living in low- and middle-income countries. The GICC was established in 2018 with the aim of increasing the survival rate, while reducing children's suffering and improving their quality of life. By 2023, cancer centers had been established in 12 countries.

CARDIOVASCULAR DISEASES

Cardiovascular diseases (CVDs) are a group of NCDs affecting the heart and blood vessels. The four main CVDs are coronary heart disease, stroke, peripheral arterial disease, and aortic disease. Together, they are the world's leading cause of death, costing around 17.9 million lives each year. Of these, 85 percent are a result of heart attacks and strokes.

Causes

Coronary heart disease occurs when the flow of oxygen-rich blood to the heart is blocked or reduced. The blockage begins with a build-up of fatty deposits on the inner walls of the blood vessels. This is called plaque. If the plaque bursts, a blood clot forms. A blood clot is a clump of semi-solid blood, and if it blocks the flow of blood to the heart, it will trigger a heart attack. When a blood clot prevents blood from reaching the brain, it causes a stroke.

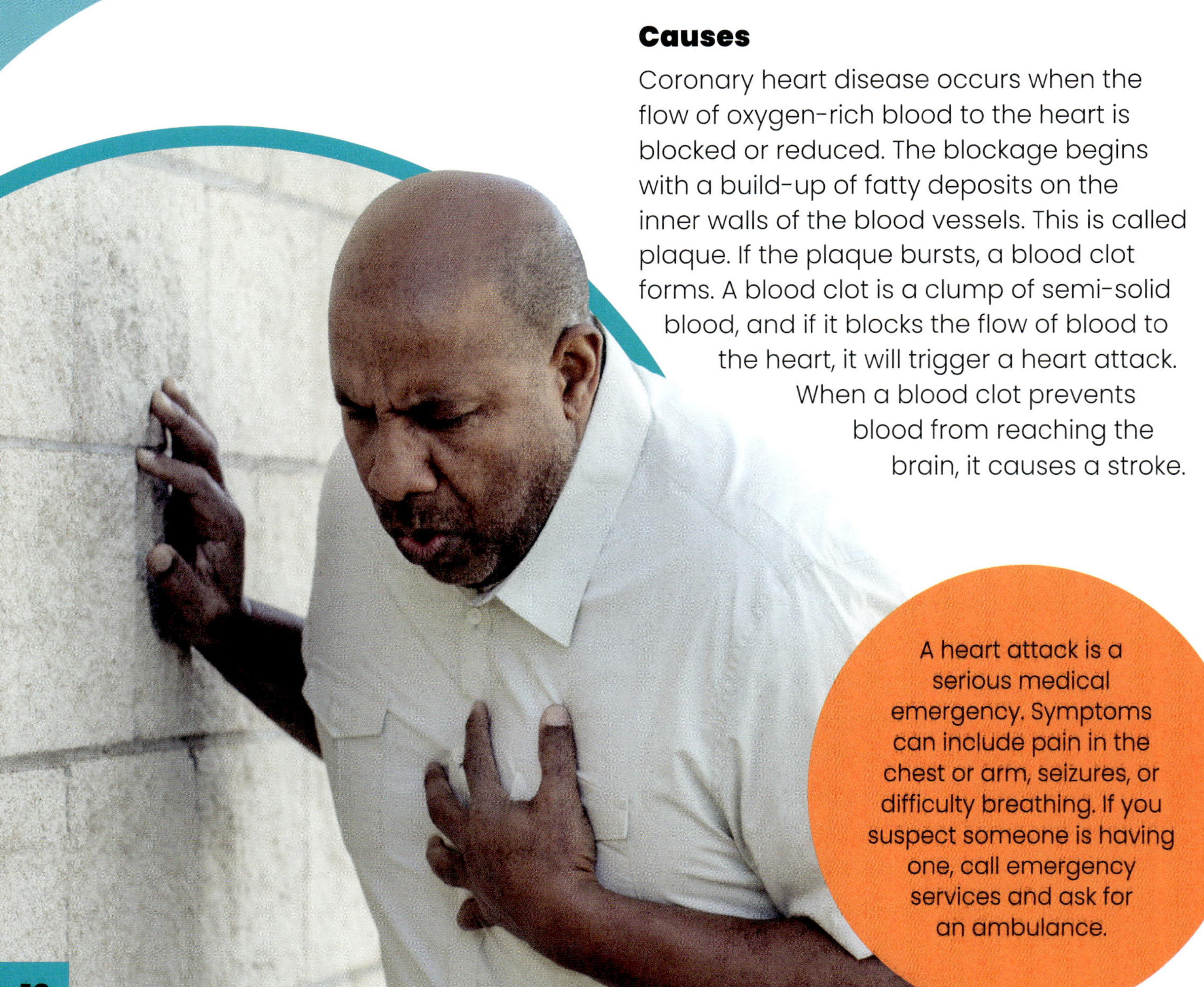

A heart attack is a serious medical emergency. Symptoms can include pain in the chest or arm, seizures, or difficulty breathing. If you suspect someone is having one, call emergency services and ask for an ambulance.

Plaque

Plaque builds up due to smoking, drinking too much alcohol, or a poor diet. People with high cholesterol (a waxy, fat-like substance found in the blood and cells), high blood pressure, and high blood sugar are also more at risk of getting a build-up of plaque.

Treatment and prevention

People with a CVD can control the disease with medicines such as aspirin, beta-blockers, and statins. To treat coronary heart disease, surgery is often required. A coronary artery bypass diverts blood around clogged parts of the arteries to improve blood flow. A balloon angioplasty involves inserting a balloon-like device through an artery to open a blockage. In the most extreme cases, patients may need a heart transplant.

The best way of preventing CVDs is to avoid smoking and alcohol, reduce salt intake, eat more fruit, vegetables, and whole grain foods, and exercise regularly.

IT'S A FACT

In 1990, around 285 million people were living with CVDs across the world. Today, that number is 550 million, an increase of 93 percent.

A defibrillator sends an electric pulse to the heart to restore a normal heartbeat. Defibrillators save hundreds of lives each year. They are often found in public places such as railway stations and shopping centers.

CHRONIC RESPIRATORY DISEASES

Chronic respiratory diseases (CRDs) affect the body's lungs and airways. The two most common CRDs are asthma and chronic obstructive pulmonary disease (COPD). CRDs are most likely to affect people exposed to tobacco smoke (both smokers and those breathing in second-hand smoke), air pollution, and dusts and chemicals in the workplace.

Asthma

Asthma affects people of all ages. It can be triggered by many things, including dust, smoke, pollen, and animal fur. This inflames and narrows the airways in the lungs, making the sufferer cough, wheeze, and feel short of breath.

Jackie Joyner-Kersee is a former US track and field athlete. She overcame severe asthma to achieve great success, winning three Olympic gold medals.

You are more likely to suffer from asthma if family members have it, if you have other allergies, such as hay fever, and if you are exposed to air pollution. There is no cure for asthma, but it can be controlled with an inhaler that supplies medication, and people with asthma can lead a healthy, active life.

Using a spacer makes it easier to use an inhaler, especially for children or during emergencies.

COPD

COPD is caused by long-term exposure to tobacco smoke or dust, fumes, and chemicals. This can narrow or block the small passages of the lungs, making it hard to breathe. The airways may also become inflamed or clogged with mucus, causing a bad cough, often called chronic bronchitis. COPD is the third-leading cause of death worldwide, with 3.23 million deaths in 2019. There is no cure for COPD, but early diagnosis and treatment helps slow the symptoms. Inhaled medications help control the disease.

HEALTHY LUNGS FOR LIFE

The Healthy Lungs for Life campaign aims to raise awareness of the importance of clean air, physical exercise, and quitting smoking. It offers advice on how to exercise with a lung condition and provides information on outdoor and indoor air pollution. People can sign up for a monthly newsletter with the latest news on treatments for lung disease.

Research suggests that exposure to air pollution can increase the risk of COPD and asthma.

DIABETES

Diabetes is a chronic NCD affecting people of all ages. Over time, if left untreated, it can cause serious damage to many of the body's systems, especially the nerves and blood vessels. Around 422 million people in the world have diabetes, and some 1.5 million people die from it each year.

Causes and symptoms

We all need glucose (sugar) in our blood for energy. Our bodies produce a substance called insulin, which controls the amount of glucose in the blood. If you have diabetes, the body doesn't produce enough or any insulin, and the amount of glucose in the blood gets too high.

There are two main types of diabetes. With type 1, the body can't make any insulin at all. Type 1 usually starts in childhood and is thought to be caused by an autoimmune reaction (the body attacking itself). With type 2, the body can't produce enough insulin or the insulin it produces doesn't work very well.

People with diabetes can check their blood glucose levels using a glucometer.

Fresh fruit and vegetables are good for diabetics because they help regulate blood sugar.

Type 2 diabetes

Type 2 is the most common type of diabetes and usually develops in adults. You're more at risk of type 2 diabetes if you are overweight or obese, if there is diabetes in your family, if you belong to certain ethnic groups, or if you have a history of high blood pressure.

Living with diabetes

If you have type 1 diabetes, you will need to take insulin regularly by injection or by using a pump. Some with type 2 diabetes will need to take insulin; others may be able to manage their diabetes and reduce its severity by healthy eating, being more active, and keeping to a healthy weight.

What Can I Do?

To reduce the risk of type 2 diabetes, include more fruit and vegetables in your diet. Foods that are known to be particularly good for this are apples, grapes, berries, and green leafy vegetables, including spinach, kale, arugala, and watercress.

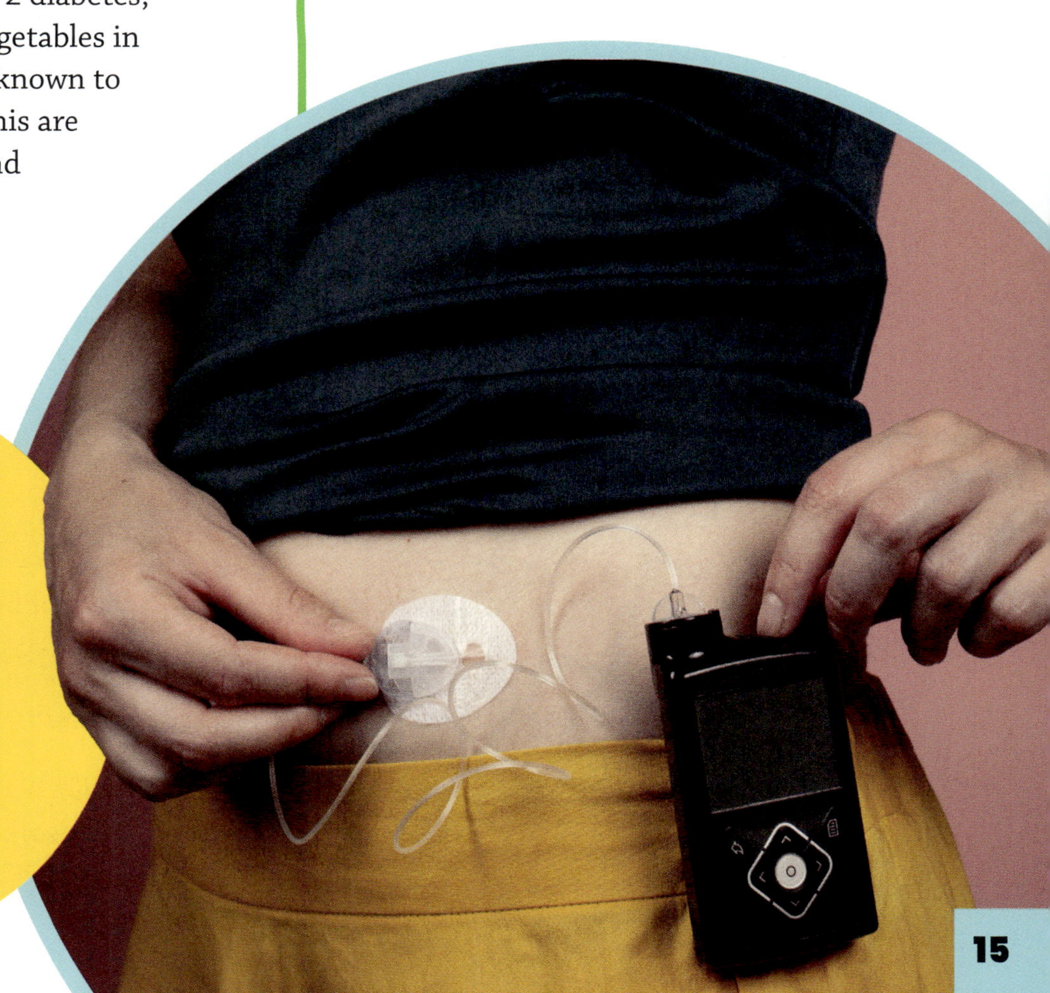

People can manage their type 1 diabetes with an insulin pump that drip-feeds insulin into the body. They can deliver larger doses when needed, such as before meals.

COMMUNICABLE DISEASES

Communicable diseases are diseases that spread from one living thing to another. We can catch communicable diseases from other people, from animals, or from microorganisms (tiny living things) in our food or on a surface.

Causes

Communicable diseases are caused by harmful microorganisms, also known as pathogens. The four main kinds are bacteria, viruses, parasites, and fungi. These pathogens will infect a "host," such as a human or animal, and the host then spreads the disease.

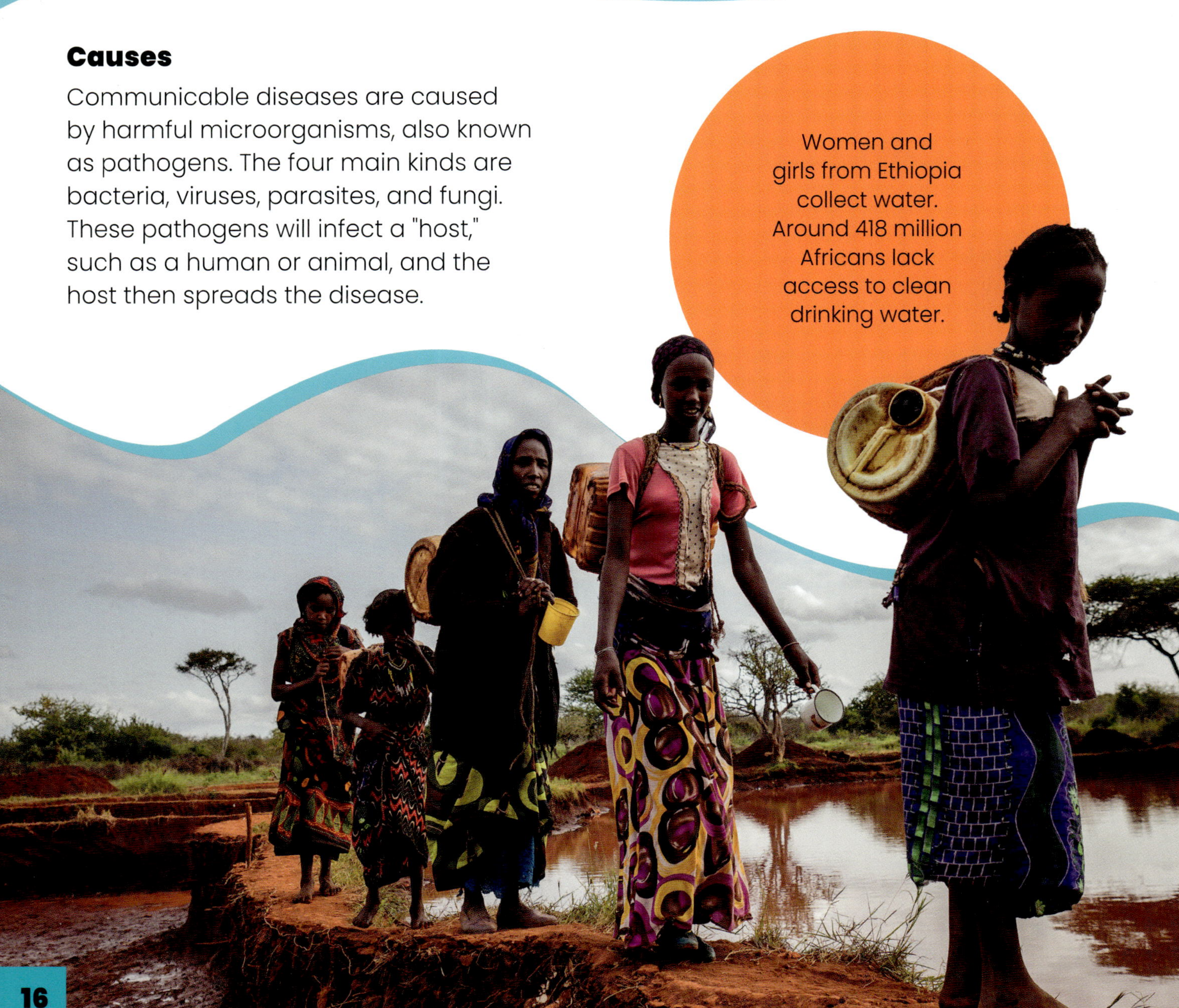

Women and girls from Ethiopia collect water. Around 418 million Africans lack access to clean drinking water.

Transmission

Diseases can spread through the air if the host sneezes or coughs and others breathe in the pathogen. They can also spread through contact with a host's skin, blood, or bodily fluids, such as saliva. Some diseases can spread indirectly, when someone comes into contact with an object, food, or water contaminated by a host.

Communicable diseases spread easily in large cities where lots of people live close together. Cholera, for example, spreads where there is poor sanitation (access to clean water and sewage disposal). When human waste ends up in the water supply, drinking water may be contaminated by the cholera bacterium.

Epidemics and pandemics

As populations live with a communicable disease, their bodies naturally develop a resistance to it. Sometimes, however, a new strain (variety) of the pathogen will emerge, which people lack resistance to, and the disease can spread rapidly through the population. This is an epidemic.

If the epidemic spreads at an accelerating rate, with more cases each day than the day before, and expands to different countries, it is known as a pandemic. The most recent pandemic to impact the world is the Covid-19 pandemic.

What Can I Do?

To protect yourself from communicable diseases, handle and prepare food safely; regularly disinfect surfaces in the bathroom and kitchen; wash your hands often; cough and sneeze into a tissue or the crook of your elbow; don't share personal items like toothbrushes or towels; never touch wild animals; and stay home when sick.

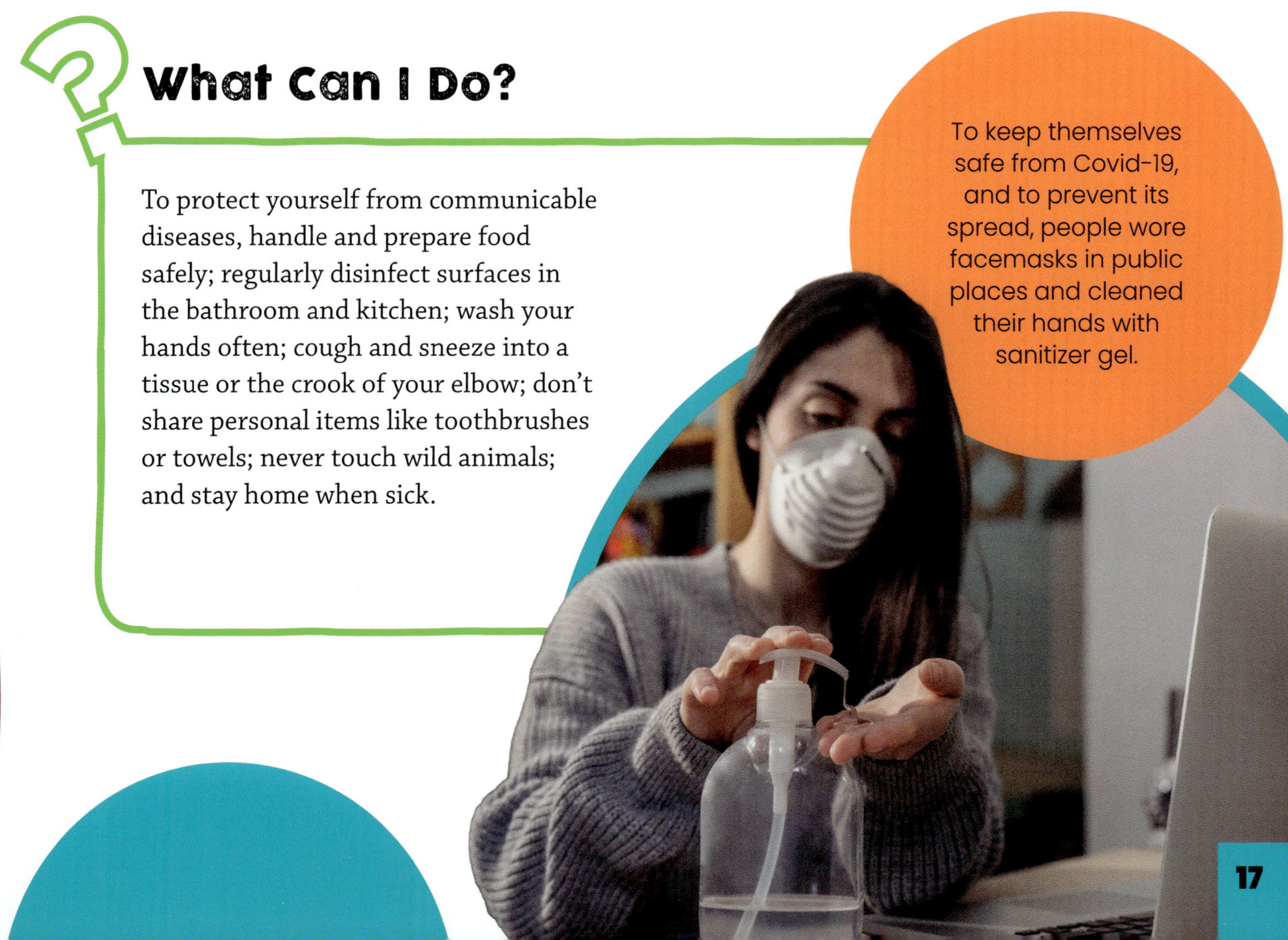

To keep themselves safe from Covid-19, and to prevent its spread, people wore facemasks in public places and cleaned their hands with sanitizer gel.

VIRAL DISEASES

Viruses are microscopic living things that can only thrive and multiply inside a host. They sometimes cause diseases, known as viral diseases. Common viral diseases include colds, the flu, and human papillomavirus. Viruses can also cause more serious illnesses such as HIV, Ebola, and Covid-19.

Causes

Most viral diseases are communicable– they can be passed on to other living things. They pass between humans through coughing, sneezing, or close contact, from contaminated food or water, from surfaces an infected person has touched, or through the bite of an infected animal.

Viruses don't have cells and cannot reproduce (make more of themselves) alone. Once inside a host, the virus takes over the host's cells and uses the "machinery" of the cells to make copies of itself. This is what makes us sick.

The Covid-19 virus looks like this under a microscope. Viruses are made up of a piece of genetic material inside a protective coating. The genetic material instructs host cells how to make more copies of the virus.

Treatments

Viral diseases such as colds rarely cause serious illness and can usually be treated by staying home for a few days, drinking lots of fluids, and getting plenty of rest. Serious viral diseases, such as Covid-19, hepatitis B and C, and HIV, can be treated with antiviral medications. These stop viruses from making copies of themselves.

Some viral diseases can be treated with convalescent plasma treatment. Someone who has recovered from the virus donates their blood. Part of the blood, called plasma, is given to the patient. This contains antibodies (see p. 24) that can help the patient fight the infection.

A former patient who has recovered from Covid-19 donates their blood for convalescent plasma treatment.

What Can I Do?

To avoid catching a viral disease, wash your hands frequently, especially during cold and flu season; store food properly, cook meat and poultry thoroughly before eating, and keep food preparation surfaces clean; protect yourself from insect bites; and never handle wild animals. Older and more vulnerable people can lower the risk of catching the flu by getting a yearly vaccine (see pp. 24–25).

To avoid passing on colds and the flu, always cover your nose and mouth when you sneeze. If you don't have a tissue, sneeze into the crook of your elbow.

BACTERIAL DISEASES

Bacteria are single-celled organisms. They are bigger than viruses and do not require a host in order to reproduce. Most bacteria aren't harmful. We have many in our body, for example helping us digest food. However, some bacteria cause disease. Examples of bacterial disease are whooping cough, cellulitis, strep throat, *E. coli*, and pneumonia. Many bacterial diseases are communicable.

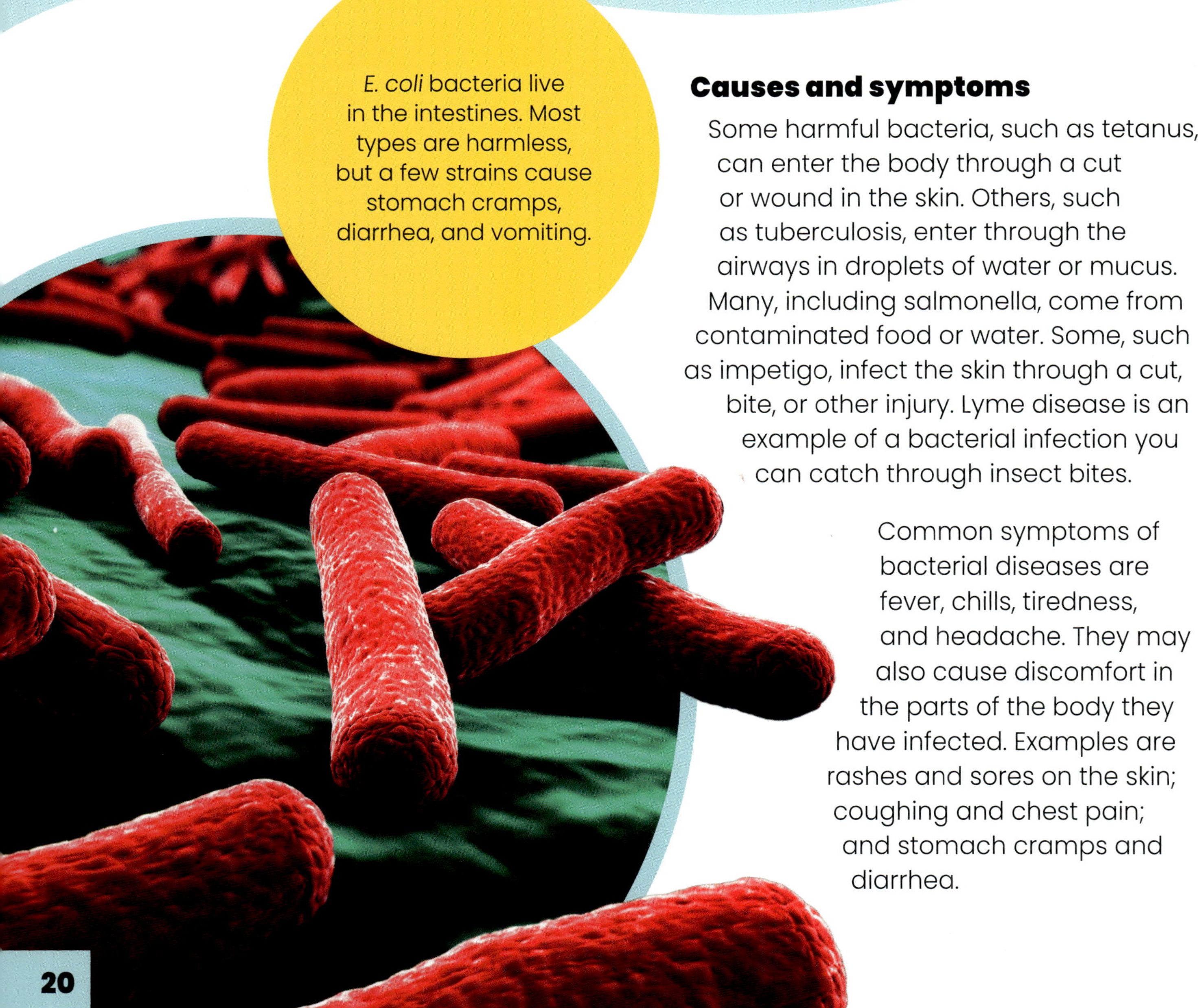

E. coli bacteria live in the intestines. Most types are harmless, but a few strains cause stomach cramps, diarrhea, and vomiting.

Causes and symptoms

Some harmful bacteria, such as tetanus, can enter the body through a cut or wound in the skin. Others, such as tuberculosis, enter through the airways in droplets of water or mucus. Many, including salmonella, come from contaminated food or water. Some, such as impetigo, infect the skin through a cut, bite, or other injury. Lyme disease is an example of a bacterial infection you can catch through insect bites.

Common symptoms of bacterial diseases are fever, chills, tiredness, and headache. They may also cause discomfort in the parts of the body they have infected. Examples are rashes and sores on the skin; coughing and chest pain; and stomach cramps and diarrhea.

Sir Alexander Fleming (1881–1955) is the physician who discovered penicillin.

ANTIBIOTICS

In 1928, Scottish scientist Alexander Fleming discovered antibiotics by accident. Returning from vacation to his lab at St. Mary's Hospital, London, he found mold on a petri dish had killed the surrounding bacteria. The active substance within the mold, penicillin, became the first antibiotic. Mass production of penicillin began around ten years later. It is estimated to have saved around 200 million lives so far.

Treatments

Some bacterial diseases don't need to be treated and will go away on their own. Others are treated with antibiotics. These are medicines that either kill bacteria or stop them multiplying. This helps the body's natural immune system to fight the infection. Antibiotics can be taken as pills, injection, an ointment or cream (for skin infections), or eye drops (for eye infections).

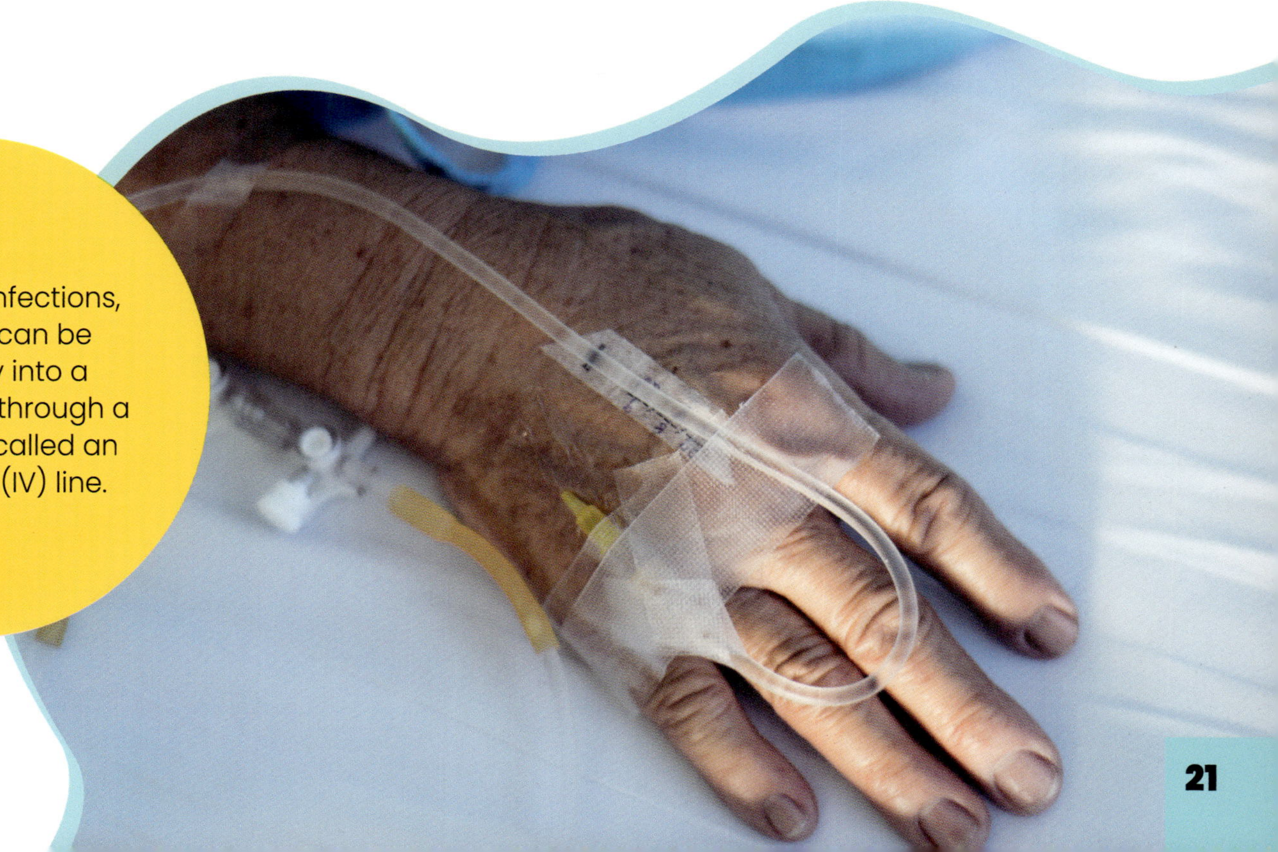

With severe infections, antibiotics can be put directly into a patient's vein through a flexible tube called an intravenous (IV) line.

PARASITIC DISEASES

Parasites are creatures that live off other living things, or hosts. Some parasites live within their hosts without causing them any noticeable harm. Others grow and reproduce within their hosts, sometimes invading other parts of their bodies. The result is a parasitic disease.

Types of parasite

Three kinds of parasite are responsible for parasitic diseases. Protozoa are tiny, single-celled creatures that can live and multiply inside the body. Helminths are larger creatures with long, flat, or round bodies that live either inside or outside the body. They include flatworms, tapeworms, and roundworms. Ectoparasites are creatures that live on or feed off the skin and include mosquitoes, fleas, ticks, and mites.

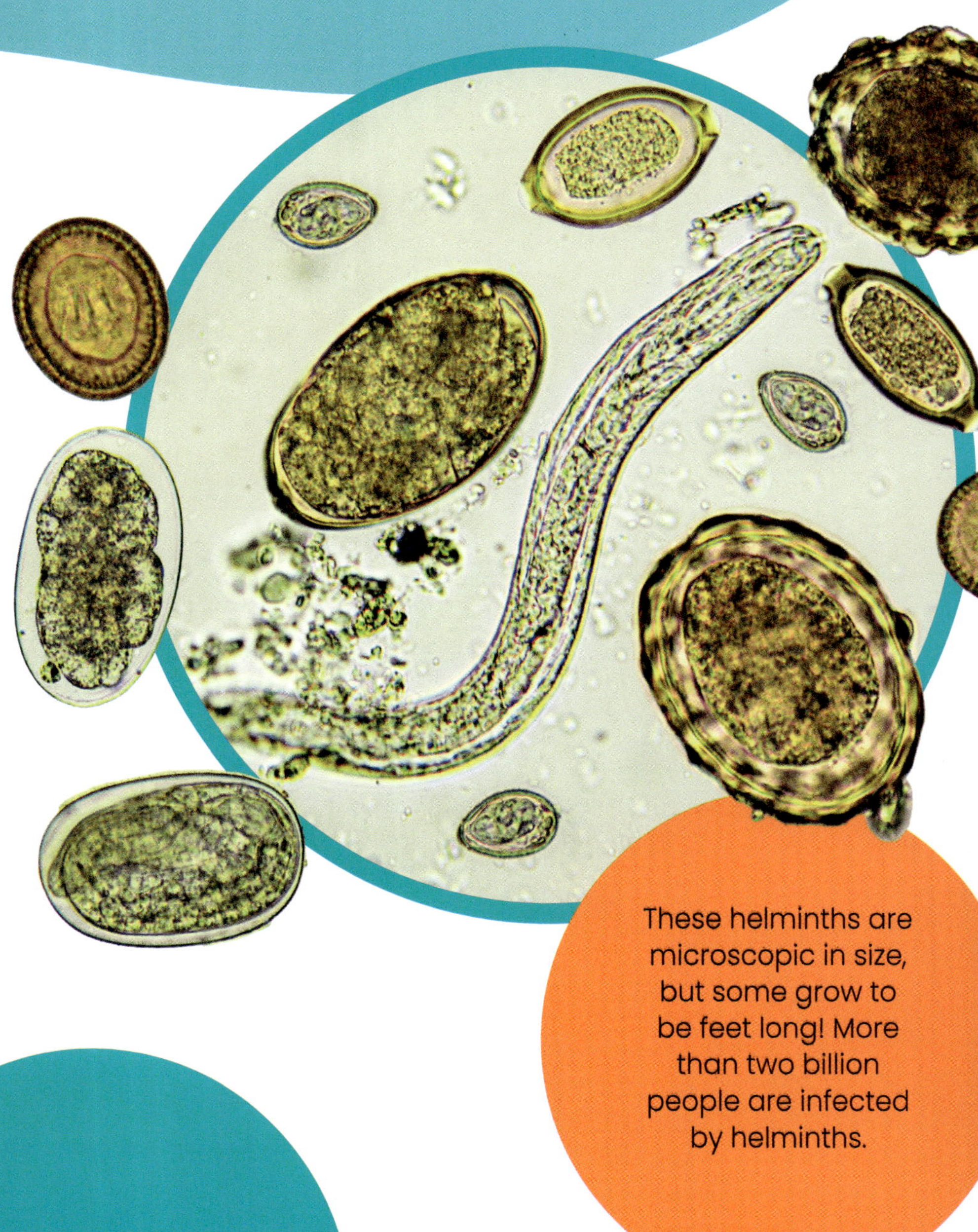

These helminths are microscopic in size, but some grow to be feet long! More than two billion people are infected by helminths.

Causes

Parasitic diseases can spread through contaminated food, water, waste, or blood. Tapeworm infection can be caught from eating undercooked meat or fish. Toxoplasmosis can be caught from food or water contaminated by cat feces. Other parasitic diseases are spread by insects that act as a vector, or carrier, of the parasite. Malaria is caused by a protozoa that enters the host through the bite of a mosquito.

Treatment and prevention

Some parasitic diseases, such as the intestinal infection giardiasis, will usually go away on their own. Others require medication to kill the parasite. In some cases of roundworm infections, surgery may be required to remove the worm if it causes a blockage in the intestines. To protect yourself from parasitic diseases, wash your hands regularly, especially after handling uncooked food or going to the toilet; cook meat and fish thoroughly; and avoid cat litter and feces. In tropical places, cover the skin and use insect repellant.

MALARIA

Since 2000, governments and charitable organizations have spent billions in the fight against malaria, with the ultimate aim of eradicating this disease. Millions of lives have been saved thanks to the provision of insecticide-treated bed nets, rapid diagnosis, effective medicines, and better access to treatment.

Insecticide-treated bed nets have dramatically reduced the risk of people catching malaria.

VACCINATION

A vaccine is a substance designed to protect us from bacterial and viral diseases. It helps our immune system – our body's natural defenses – to build resistance against infection. Thanks to vaccination, millions of lives have been saved, and one disease, smallpox, has been completely eradicated.

Lymphocytes and antibodies

Cells in our bodies called lymphocytes are activated by the presence of pathogens (see p. 16). Lymphocytes identify them as pathogens because they carry markers called antigens. Some lymphocytes attack the invaders directly. Others make substances called antibodies to destroy them. During the time it takes to make the antibodies, we can get sick. After fighting off the infection, antibodies remain in our blood. If the infection returns, they fight it off quickly before it can make us sick. In other words, we build up an immunity.

How vaccines work

Vaccines contain dead or weakened forms of a particular virus or bacterium. These cannot harm us, but they train our immune system to recognize the pathogen from its antigen and produce antibodies to fight it off. If we become exposed to the disease in future, the antibodies will destroy the pathogen before it can make us unwell.

Vaccines go through careful preparation and testing to ensure they are safe before being made available to the public.

How long do vaccines last?

Our immune system has a long memory and, once vaccinated against a disease such as measles, we remain protected for life. For other diseases, like the flu, we need a new vaccine each year because different flu strains (varieties) emerge.

Why vaccination is important

Getting vaccinated protects not only ourselves but those around us. Some people cannot be vaccinated, including people who are very sick or have severe allergies. They depend on others being vaccinated against diseases to ensure they, too, are safe from them.

THE COVAX INITIATIVE

COVAX was a global effort to ensure that all countries, including poorer ones, have equal access to Covid-19 vaccines. Led by UNICEF, COVAX began distributing vaccines in February 2021. By November 2022, 1.8 billion doses had been delivered to 146 countries. It was the largest vaccine operation in history.

Most vaccines are given by injection. Vaccination is safe and side effects are usually minor and temporary.

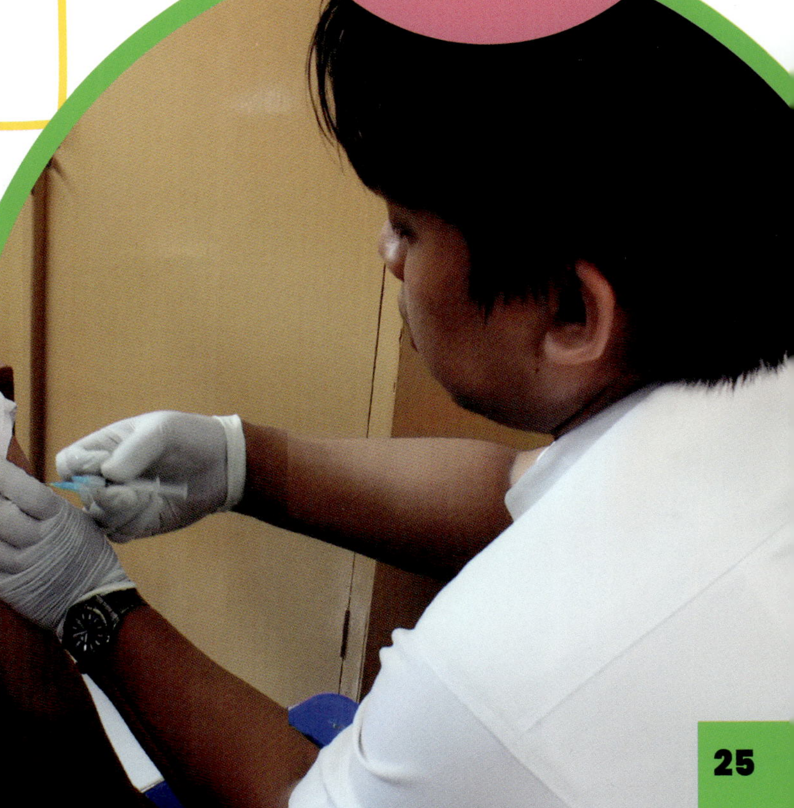

PUBLIC HEALTH AND SANITATION

Diseases affect communities as well as individuals, and governments can help fight disease by passing laws that promote the health of the population as a whole. Public health can also be improved through educational campaigns, control of infections, and providing decent sanitation.

Laws and campaigns

Governments can pass laws to ensure, for example, that foods sold in shops meet basic health standards, or that factories are not able to pollute the environment with their emissions. Governments and charities often launch campaigns to raise public awareness of health issues. Campaigns might encourage people to exercise more, eat more fruit and vegetables, give up smoking, get vaccinated, or get screened for cancer.

A public health official in a hospital in Thailand gives advice to patients after being vaccinated against Covid-19.

Control of infections

In an epidemic or pandemic, governments will act to control the spread of the disease. They may pass laws to enforce social distancing between people. Public and private gatherings may be banned, and schools and workplaces may have to close. People who test positive for the disease are told to self-isolate until they are no longer infectious.

Sanitation

Over 1.7 billion people around the world lack basic sanitation, such as toilets or latrines. The problem is particularly acute for poor people in low- and middle-income countries, where sewage systems are limited or non-existent and many are forced to defecate outdoors. Poor sanitation can lead to diseases such as cholera, dysentery, and parasitic worm infections. The World Health Organization is leading global efforts to improve sanitation in poor countries and aims to eliminate open defecation by 2030.

What Can I Do?

About 771 million people in the world live without clean water. Most live in rural areas and must spend hours each day walking to collect water, which is often not clean. You can help by getting involved with a charity that helps provide clean, safe water to people around the world. You could launch a fundraising campaign, make a monthly donation, or sponsor a project.

Houses on stilts rise above the polluted water in this city in Peru. People here have little or no access to clean water or sanitation.

THE FUTURE OF DISEASE

The threat of disease will always be with us and is forever changing. New strains of communicable diseases will emerge. Obesity and alcohol consumption are on the rise, which will take a toll on our health. But science is also advancing, and we are finding new ways of fighting disease.

Antibiotics can be overused and misused, causing some bacteria to become resistant to them. This bacterium, MRSA, has become a major cause of illness in hospitals.

Challenges

As the climate warms, tropical and subtropical diseases, such as malaria, are likely to take hold in new areas. More and more people will live close together in cities. This, along with increasing global travel, will mean a greater chance of epidemics and pandemics.

Worldwide obesity has nearly tripled since 1975, and in 2019 there were 38.2 million children under five who were overweight or obese. Consequently, we are likely to see increases in cardiovascular disease and diabetes.

Climate change causes more frequent extreme weather events such as flooding, which increases the risk of waterborne diseases like cholera.

New technologies

Artificial intelligence (AI) programs will increasingly help doctors diagnose diseases and suggest treatment plans. AI is already being used to analyze scans of our insides for early signs of cancer or heart disease, and to research new medicines.

In the future, more and more people will monitor their own health with wearable devices like smartwatches, or by implants inside their bodies. These will alert them to the need for lifestyle changes and provide early warning systems for diseases like diabetes.

NEW VACCINES

The Covid-19 pandemic sparked a massive drive to create a vaccine, and several effective vaccines were created in record time. Among them was a kind of vaccine using a molecule called messenger RNA (mRNA). Scientists are now developing vaccines based on this method to protect against other diseases such as malaria, dengue fever, Zika, Ebola, rabies, HIV, and even certain kinds of cancer.

Smartwatches can track things like physical fitness, sleep patterns, heart rate, and blood pressure.

GLOSSARY

allergy A damaging response by the body's immune system to a substance.

antibiotic A medicine that hinders the growth of or destroys bacteria.

antibody A substance produced in the blood to attack a particular antigen.

artery Any of the muscular-walled blood vessels that supplies blood from the heart to all parts of the body.

bacterium (plural: bacteria) A member of a large group of single-celled micro-organisms, some of which cause disease.

cardiovascular Relating to the heart and blood vessels.

chronic (of an illness) Lasting for a long time or constantly recurring.

coronary Relating to the arteries that surround the heart and supply it with blood.

defecate Discharge feces (poop) from the body.

diagnose Identify an illness by examining the symptoms.

epidemic A widespread outbreak of an infectious disease.

feces (poop) Waste matter that is discharged from the body.

fungus (plural: fungi) A group of organisms, including molds, yeast, and mushrooms, some of which cause disease.

genetic Relating to genes. Genes are units within your body's cells that carry information inherited from your parents and determine your features or characteristics.

host A person, animal, or plant on which a parasite or microorganism lives.

immune system The network of organs, tissues, and cells within the body that protect it from disease.

implant A device or object placed inside the body.

lymphatic system Lymph is a colorless fluid containing white blood cells that bathes the tissues. It flows through a network of vessels called the lymphatic system into the blood.

molecule A group of atoms.

mucus A slimy substance secreted by people and animals for lubrication.

pandemic A very widespread outbreak of an infectious disease that spreads at an accelerating rate across several countries or the whole world.

parasite A living thing that lives on or inside another living thing (its host), taking nourishment from the host at the host's expense.

pathogen A bacterium, virus, or other microorganism that can cause disease.

pollen A fine, powdery substance discharged from flowers. It can cause allergies in some people.

pulmonary Relating to the lungs.

respiratory Relating to breathing and the organs used for breathing.

sanitation The provision of clean drinking water and adequate sewage disposal.

strain A particular variety of an animal, plant, or microorganism.

tissue Any of the individual types of material of which our bodies are made, made up of particular kinds of cell.

UNICEF The United Nations Children's Fund works to improve the health and education of children and their mothers.

virus A microscopic living thing that can only multiply within the cells of a host, and sometimes cause diseases.

World Health Organization An agency established in 1948 to promote health and control diseases.

FURTHER INFORMATION

Books

Deadly Diseases by Robin Twiddy, Bearport Publishing, 2024

Pandemic Planet: How Diseases Impact Our World (And What You Can Do To Help Stop Their Spread) by Anna Claybourne, Franklin Watts, 2022

Why We Need Vaccines: How Humans Beat Infectious Diseases by Rowena Rae, Orca Book Publishers, 2024

Websites

www.bbc.co.uk/bitesize/guides/z9dhjty/revision/1
Learn about non-communicable diseases, their causes, effects, and risk factors.

www.nhs.uk/conditions/
The website of the National Health Service contains hundreds of articles on diseases, describing signs and symptoms, how to reduce your risk, and what treatments are available.

www.who.int/
The website of the World Health Organization contains fact sheets, symptoms, treatments, prevention strategies, and the latest news on all the major diseases.

INDEX